CPA MARKETING

How CPA Marketing Is Making Average People Millionaires

Jerry Shoemaker

DISCLAIMER

The information contained in "CPA MARKETING," and its components, is meant to serve as a comprehensive collection of strategies that the author of this eBook has done research about. Summaries, strategies, tips and tricks are only recommendations by the author, and reading this eBook will not guarantee that one's results will exactly mirror the author's results.

The author of this Ebook has made all reasonable efforts to provide current and accurate information for the readers of this eBook. The author and its associates will not be held liable for any unintentional errors or omissions that may be found.

The material in the Ebook may include information by third parties. Third party materials comprise of opinions expressed by their owners. As such, the author of this eBook does not assume responsibility or liability for any third party material or opinions.

The publication of third party material does not constitute the author's guarantee of any information, products, services, or opinions contained within third party material. Use of third party material does not guarantee that your results will mirror our results. Publication of such third party material is simply a recommendation and expression of the author's own opinion of that material.

Whether because of the progression of the Internet, or the unforeseen changes in company policy and editorial submission guidelines, what is stated as fact at the time of this writing may become outdated or inapplicable later.

This Ebook is copyright ©2017 by Jerry Shoemaker with all rights reserved. It is illegal to redistribute, copy, or create derivative works from this Ebook whole or in parts. No parts of this report may be reproduced or retransmitted in any forms whatsoever without the written expressed and signed permission from the author.

TABLE OF CONTENTS

DISCLAIMER

TABLE OF CONTENTS

INTRODUCTION

CHAPTER 1: WHAT IS CPA - A COMPREHENSIVE EXPLANATION

CHAPTER 2: HOW TO SELECT THE RIGHT CPA OFFER

   How to Study the Market Competition

   How do you compare CPA offers?

CHAPTER 3: METHODS OF PROMOTING CPA OFFERS

CHAPTER 4: HOW TO SELECT CPA OFFERS

CHAPTER 5: THE TOP 8 CPA NETWORKS TO JOIN

1. MaxBounty
2. AdCombo
3. PeerFly
4. CPALead
5. ClickDealer
6. CPABuild
7. Wild Affiliates
8. Ibex Network

CHAPTER 6: TRAFFIC TACTICS

   FREE TRAFFIC

      Natural Search Traffic

      Social Media Traffic

      Forum Traffic

      Article Writing Traffic

      Domain Name Traffic

      Reciprocal Linking Traffic

      Blogging Traffic

      Joint Venture Traffic

      Pop Up Traffic

      Video Traffic

      Podcast Traffic

      Software Traffic

      Facebook Applications Traffic

- PAID TRAFFIC
  - Pay Per Click Search Engine Traffic
  - Publisher Network Traffic
  - Text Link Traffic
  - Co-Registration Traffic
  - Banner Traffic
  - Media Buys Traffic
- RECYCLED TRAFFIC
  - Email Traffic
  - Internal Banner Traffic
  - Forum Recycled Traffic
  - Surveys and Poll Traffic
- VIRAL TRAFFIC
  - Pillar #1: Innovative Product or Service
  - Pillar #2: Ease of Transfer
  - Pillar #3: Motivational Factor
  - Pillar #4: Third-Party Resources
  - Pillar #5: Scalability
  - Social Networking Traffic
  - Tell A Friend Script Traffic
  - Viral Report Traffic

CHAPTER 7: WHY DO SO MANY CPA AFFILIATE MARKETERS FAIL?
- You Quit Too Soon – It's Also What CPA Marketers Do Far Too Often
- Running before You Walk
- Is Your CPA Marketing Actually Working?
- CPA Marketing Done Right Means Success

CHAPTER 8: 6 STEPS TO CHOOSE THE BEST CPA OFFER TO PROMOTE
- Step #1
- Step #2
- Step #3
- Step #4
- Step #5
- Step #6

CHAPTER 9: HOW TO JOIN A CPA NETWORK

CHAPTER 10: THE #1 FEAR IN CPA MARKETING

CHAPTER 11: THE BENEFITS OF CPA MARKETING

Why Use CPA Marketing

CONCLUSION

INTRODUCTION

In a world of information overload and misinformation, I am confident that this eBook will give you a clear understanding of how CPA marketing and the CPA industry works, regardless of the fact that you are a novice or you've been in the game for years. The biggest challenge that you will encounter in the CPA marketing game is traffic and time. Contrary to what you have heard or read, playing the CPA marketing game is not as easy as it appears. It takes a lot of hard work, dedication and persistence to make a lot of money with CPA offers.

The CPA market is nothing new and has been around since the mid 1990's and brokering traffic from traffic sources like pay per click search engines to CPA offers has been a business for many affiliates for the last ten years

Nowadays, in the field of internet or online marketing, 'affiliate marketing' is a popular term. In affiliate marketing, affiliates can earn money by promoting the products or services of other people or companies in return for a commission on the number of sales made. But have you heard about the new type of affiliate marketing where people get paid even if they don't make a sale?

Yes, it is true. Well, it has been possible by a new wave of affiliate marketing flowing through the web, known as 'CPA Affiliate Marketing' or just "CPA Marketing'. Now, you can earn money online with CPA Marketing.

This eBook is a comprehensive guide for anyone looking to learn more about what CPA Marketing and earning from the affiliate program.

CHAPTER 1: WHAT IS CPA - A COMPREHENSIVE EXPLANATION

CPA, which stands for Cost per Action, is basically a form of affiliate advertisement that is used by almost all companies throughout the world to generate leads for their products. This marketing is done by affiliates who work through their own websites in order to send traffic to the advertiser's website for the product of the company. CPA deals with specific forms of marketing which involve pay per click and pay per lead ads.

Although Google used CPA networking as a major part of their advertising campaign till June 2008, eBay has now taken up this form of marketing and calls it AdContext. CPA is also known as Cost per Acquisition. This makes more sense literally, since affiliate advertisers under CPA networks are paid based on what the advertiser acquires from his or her customers. There is no returning of funds in this sort of advertisement. As long as the entire action is completed by potential customers, affiliates get paid per lead that they provide to the advertiser. This makes it easier and simpler for advertisers to work for their company, as well as for affiliates to work for their advertisers.

Since there are many CPA networks out there and hundreds of affiliates are hired from these networks, advertisers usually have affiliate managers who go through the resume of each of these affiliates and hire only those who have the best lead generation records, or are the most appropriate for a specific line of marketing.

The basic deal with CPA marketing is to generate traffic to the company's website. This job is outsourced by the advertisers of these companies to the affiliates, who in turn get paid in commission depending on the quality of lead generation that they can provide. Affiliates then use various forms of advertising such as banner ads, keywords, article directories, pay per click ads and video ads to attract more traffic for the website.

Companies that sell insurance, credit and/or debit cards, public bonds or even ring tones of cell phones, use CPA networks to build their leads. Affiliates should stay in touch with their managers since the latter are well informed about the latest information regarding the CPA networks and the newest ideas for this sort of marketing.

Although getting paid $30 for each action that an affiliate is able to generate from potential customers may seem like a cheap bargain for the work that they go through, if they have a handsome customer profile of about 400 to 500, then this amount can multiply into a hefty pay packet per month.

CHAPTER 2: HOW TO SELECT THE RIGHT CPA OFFER

Once you've been selected by a CPA network, you will need to start to make choices relating to the offers that you are attracted to selling to your online customers. Don't make your choice based just on your likes and dislikes, which means you will need to find the niches that sell more, and that direct high amounts of traffic to enjoy making the huge bucks.

How to Study the Market Competition

The main facet of any business success is the creative intelligence. It really isn't just about who you know, working exhaustively, or luck. No matter what you do, you should always be at your creative best. To be at your best with CPA marketing, you need to do an overload of research to learn what keywords always hit big in the search engines and the ones that are always popular, and you need to watch out for the well-known niches using the many trend sites. Once you know the keywords that are searched extensively. This means that they haven't been used in CPA offers yet, and so you can grab them to use to create your own advertisements for sales.

When you learn that a certain CPA offer is very popular, don't make the mistake of thinking it means that it's a dead end for you. Instead, use the information you've found to get a better understanding of the various products that are tirelessly wanted, and then use them to generate traffic on your website.

The key is to utilize the same methods, the same materials, and the same taglines in making the sales. What matters more than what you sell is how you sell it. There is a huge difference. Your creativity needs to come to forefront and you need to come up with quirky ideas that will appeal to the online shopper.

How do you compare CPA offers?

The main CPA mantra is that your choices should be the ones that are hot, trendy, popular and highest in demand. If you can find that with CPA offers, regardless if they generate a little or a lot of traffic, whether they will fall, or not – you will be making the correct decision with less likelihood of facing defeat.

When you are trying to make the choice regarding which CPA offers you should pick to sell, instead of undertaking individually going through them, which is extremely time consuming, why not take advantage of the many online tools and programs that can quickly help you to located the information you need.

It is a misconception believing that if a CPA offer provides the highest pay then it is the right choice. This way of thinking that can lead to failure. You need to do your research find the niche product that's going to sell over and over again!

CHAPTER 3: METHODS OF PROMOTING CPA OFFERS

There are a number of ways that your CPA promotion can be done. Some of these involve you having your own website while others do not. CPA marketing is very similar to other forms of marketing. At the beginning, you will need to take some time to think about what product you can promote that will fit your niche and where you can market it, where your visitors will either be interested in learning more or in buying a product.

Let's have a look at some of the most commonly used promotional methods for CPA marketing on websites.

1. Sales or Landing Page – This is like a direct sales page and should usually provide additional information on the product. Usually, it's set up to be a hard sale, working hard to get the visitor to click through to the merchant or at least sign up to the site's mailing list. Some sales pages attempt to achieve both of these; however, often it is more beneficial to have one direct path through your landing page. If you have too many options, you could lose more clicks.

2. Review Website – This type of site usually contain three or more products in a specific niche, for instance, weight loss or gardening. There will be a brief introduction to each of the products, followed by a review of the performance of the product, and then often followed with a star rating out of five. Each product is usually ranked in order and contain a link to either a personalized landing page or directly to the merchant's page.

3. Splash Page – Generally, this contains light content with flashy graphics and a punchy headline. The copy encourages the visitors to input their details or to click through to the merchant's site. There is minimal product information provided. These kinds of pages are often used with products that don't need much explanation or that are already known in the marketplace like the iPhone.

4. Fun Landing Page – This is similar to a splash page but simpler. Generally, there is a question with two or more answers, which can be clicked on using the very large dominant buttons. Sometimes a game is used on this kind of page. It isn't the type of page that someone revisits. Its only goal is for your visitors to click-through now.

We've talked about different promotional methods on your website. Of course, there are other methods which will be discussed in the coming chapters but these are one of the most popular.

CHAPTER 4: HOW TO SELECT CPA OFFERS

Once you decide it's time to start making money with CPA Marketing, you need to browse through the many CPA offers. Start by selecting the best 8-10 CPA networks that you would like to become involved in. Doing this makes it more helpful than just trying to choose one niche and spending all kinds of time doing the research, only to discover that there are all kinds of offers available to you. You can waste a great deal of time and energy, and become more frustrated.

After you choose 8 to 10 best offers, you need to sit down and start to work your way through the markets available online to learn which are the most popular in demand, and to learn which ones are easiest to make the most money. The trick here is to learn what hot topics are being searched for the most in the search engines and news. Google trends are the best place to begin. Go to http://google.com/trends, to find personality news stories. You will need to watch so you don't become sidetracked by these stories. Avoid the personality stories because people aren't interested in personalities when they are reading about the product(s) they are interested in purchasing.

Some other trends to have a look at include:

http://www.google.com/press/zeitgeist.htm

http://hotsearches.aol.com

http://buzzlog.buzz.yahoo.com/buzzlog

http://www.blogniscient.com

After going through these trend sites, you'll have ideas about what is hot and what actually sells the most, along with which niches are closely related to your CPA offers. The best trick to use is to find a sub-niche in a larger niche related to your CPA offers. Don't be scared to make offers available in highly competitive markets. Those where most of the traffic is directed is where you'll do best.

You need to spend a couple of hours researching how you can best create a significant revenue with the CPA network niche you are considering. If you have a number of your own websites, you can continue to keep watching for better offers in the CPA networks. The domain name you use should be related to the niche you are planning to work in.

Now that you have your niche, the work you do will be done upfront. When you are building your site up, you are going to have to change the offers regularly. You may find it tiring to create different websites for different CPA offers, but those e-market affiliates who are experienced can whip up a site in just a few hours using Wordpress. If you want to make it to the top of the earning pool, you'll have to learn how to do this as well.

CHAPTER 5: THE TOP 8 CPA NETWORKS TO JOIN

If you are an affiliate marketer, the first step you need to take to earn good money through online advertising is to join as many CPA networks as possible. Different CPA networks have their own various lead programs that marketers can use. Choose those with high pay per lead and good resell options, as this will lead to higher income generation for you. 8 of the top CPA networks include:

1. MaxBounty

Running a successful CPA Affiliate Network since 2004, MaxBounty has stood the test of time and has become one of the well-known names in the industry. Now, MaxBounty is considered as one of the most popular CPA Affiliate Network. Presently it has thousands of satisfied affiliates that are earning the considerable amount of revenue doing CPA advertising. You can look forward to one of the highest paying affiliate programs from MaxBounty. With MaxBounty, you are bound to get a reliable partner for CPA Affiliate Marketing.

http://promoteam.rurl.me/maxbounty

2. AdCombo

AdCombo is one of the most recognized and fastest growing CPA Affiliate Networks. It is considered as one of the oldest players in the industry and has earned the tag of being one of the most reputed CPA Affiliate Networks. As an Affiliate, you can look forward to a whole range of products and services. They have a wide range of advertisers in different categories. It has been estimated that AdCombo pays almost $ 100M a year to affiliates. Moreover, AdCombo is one of the favorite CPA Affiliate Network for almost every 'Super Affiliate'.

http://promoteam.rurl.me/adcombo

3. PeerFly

With PeerFly, you can look forward to getting excellent affiliate management as far as CPA Affiliate Marketing is concerned. PeerFly has earned the reputation of being one of the fastest growing CPA Affiliate Network in the world. It already has more than 30k publishers spread across 165 countries around the world. As an advertiser, you can look forward to dedicated account managers and lots of other quality services. It runs various CPA offers in different categories from well-known brands. So as a CPA Affiliate you get a wide gamut of choices of affiliate programs from PeerFly.

4. CPALead

CPALead is another leading CPA Affiliate Network that has been running successfully for a considerable length of time. CPALead was previously known as CPAdverts. You can look forward to a whole range of affiliate programs from CPALead. It is a well-known name in the industry and one of the biggest companies running a CPA Affiliate Network. As an affiliate, you can have many quality services from CPALead such as timely payment of bills. Seeing its performance and deliverables in the past recent years, you can expect the CPALead network to continue to grow and flourish in the future, as well.

http://promoteam.rurl.me/cpalead

5. ClickDealer

ClickDealer is one of the greatest CPA affiliate networks, they have a lot of offers with good payout. They have some great affiliate manager who is always ready to help you. For payment, you don't have to worry as ClickDealer offer on-time payment, they also offer direct deposits. If you are looking for a good CPA affiliate network ClickDealer is a great option.

6. CPABuild

CPABuild is another trustworthy and performance driven CPA Affiliate Network coming your way. It figures among the top 10 CPA Affiliate Networks. Moreover, it has been voted as the 5th Best CPA Network so you can very well ascertain its popularity and success in CPA Affiliate Marketing. CPABuild's success springs from the fact that it has based its business on the platform of trust, integrity, respect, and honor. While keeping an eye on the latest technology, CPABuild offers a whole range of quality services to both its advertisers and publishers. You stand to benefit and increase your revenue stream by becoming an advertiser or joining in its various affiliate programs as a publisher.

http://promoteam.rurl.me/cpabuild

7. Wild Affiliates

In its small period of existence, Wild Affiliates has gained the reputation of being one of the fastest growing CPA Affiliate Networks. Moreover, it is now been recognized as one of the largest CPA Affiliate Networks for the casino niche, as well. Wild Affiliates has a whole range of excellent offers and services for its clients with utmost accuracy and dedication. With their 24/7 support team, they guarantee to resolve your queries as soon as possible. So, if you are looking for a reliable, trustworthy, and fast casino-targeted CPA Affiliate Network, then you can surely depend upon the services of Wild Affiliates.

http://promoteam.rurl.me/wildaffiliates

8. Ibex Network

Featuring among the top CPA Affiliate Networks, Ibex Network is another leading CPA Affiliate Network in the world of casino's, gambling in general and games. It has been incorporated with the sole objective of becoming a global performance-based publisher network and is successfully fulfilling its objective. Ibex Network already has thousands of publishers and is able to generate millions of leads/sales per month for its advertising clients. It offers campaigns in almost every segment of categories including top brand casino's that can be promoted through various channels such as email, mobile, social media, web, etc. It has much to offer to both advertisers and publishers. Publishers can look forward to the large gamut of offers, round the clock personalized support, and top payout among others.

http://promoteam.rurl.me/ibex

CHAPTER 6: TRAFFIC TACTICS

There are many forms of traffic that I believe fall into the following four (4) major categories which will all be covered in this section. This section isn't a complete list of all the traffic methods, but rather a quick list of the most common forms of generating traffic to CPA offers.

You can make a ton of money sending traffic to CPA offers from these four traffic models.

The four traffic models are:

- Free Traffic

- Paid Traffic

- Recycled Traffic

- Viral Traffic

Each of these traffic sources could be an entire course on its own. It is not my objective to make this report the encyclopedia of Internet marketing, but rather to point you to resources that I think can help you create traffic.

If you can learn to monetize any of these sources of traffic, you have established the first step towards online success.

FREE TRAFFIC

Natural Search Traffic

Natural search traffic is simply having your web pages indexed by major search engines such as Google, Yahoo or MSN. Back then in the late 1990's, it was very easy to get ranked in the major search engines. Today it is brutally competitive and difficult to get a high ranking for relevant keywords or key phrases.

But it is still possible through some hard work and dedication.

There are two major components to getting your web pages ranked well and they are:

1. *On Page Factors*

2. *Off Page factors*

On page, factors include where to place your keywords on your web pages and the keyword density. The obvious methods to improve your on-page factors are:

- include relevant keywords in meta tags

- include relevant keywords in your H1, H2, H3 tags

- include relevant keywords in your image tags (the alt text tag)

- include relevant keywords in your content

Off page factors include other web sites that link back to your web site. There are some things that major search engines look at when analyzing the inbound links to your web site:

- the number of inbound links

- the anchor text used to link to your web site

- the IP address of web site linking to your web site

The off-page factors accounts for 90% of how well ranked your web pages are for relevant keywords in the major search engines.

When you are exchanging links with other web sites, don't simply use your web site name, but rather a keyword that best describes what your web site is all about.

Once you have your website compiled and all the internal links working, you can submit them to the major search engines. With Google, you can use Google Sitemaps, and they will send the Google spider to index your web page right away.

You need to create a sitemap in .xml format for your web site to submit it to Google Sitemaps (*http://www.google.com/webmasters/sitemaps*).

Social Media Traffic

Social media traffic refers to taking advantage of Web 2.0 sites to generate traffic to the CPA offers that you are promoting. There are essentially two different ways that you can take advantage of Web 2.0 sites.

1. Direct Approach

2. Indirect Approach

Using the direct approach, you can link the CPA offer you are promoting right from the Web 2.0 websites. So, for example, you may create a page on HubPages.com related to home renovations, and then link to home improvement CPA offers from your hub pages.

Using the indirect approach, you use the linking power of web 2.0 websites to build quality links to your money site (the site that makes you money with CPA offers).

For a thorough guide on Social Media Marketing, check out my ebook *"Social Media Marketing: Proven Strategies To Make Big Money Online"* at this link:
https://www.amazon.com/dp/B074WGKMHR

Forum Traffic

Another method of driving traffic to your CPA offers is to participate in forums that are related to the CPA offer that you would like to promote. Most forums allow you to create a signature file, which means that this signature will be displayed at the end of every forum message that you write.

You can use this area to promote your CPA offer directly or send prospects to your money site and promote your CPA offers from there. For example, if you were promoting a "backyard makeover" CPA offer, you could start participating in forums related to gardening.

The people who are visiting this forum are your ideal prospects who will be interested in the CPA offer and are likely to fill it out.

Article Writing Traffic

Article writing and submission to major article directories is one of the most powerful methods of attracting free traffic to your web sites.

Writing articles or having articles written for your web sites can also help you get better search engine rankings and drive targeted prospects straight to your website.

Some people might start moaning and groaning since they saw "writing articles". No one is really a fan of that though, but the good news is that you can always outsource whatever writeup you want easily. You could also run Google AdSense – a win-win situation.

Now, I am not suggesting that you go "buck wild" and have thousands of articles written. You can start off with outsourcing just a few articles until you find the right article writer.

You will want to test more than one article writer because some just won't give you good quality articles. You need to dig around until you find that right person.

Once you have these articles written by yourself or outsourced, you can easily submit them to free article directories and email announcement lists. This will create some really good targeted traffic to your web site.

Articles are great traffic producers because you get free exposure for your web site. Authors are allowed to include a small biography at the bottom of the article, and this is a great place to put a link back to your web site.

If you are using HTML in your article or signature file at the end of an article, remember to use your most relevant keywords as your anchor text for your link so that you can improve your SEO rankings.

Try Fiverr to find cheap article writers: http://promoteam.rurl.me/fiverr

Domain Name Traffic

This tactic involves registering domain names that are relevant to what you are selling or promoting.

Test and studies have indicated that domain names that include keywords that are searched for have a better ranking than other websites that don't.

Most relevant keywords and keyword phrases have already been registered, but by using a cool software tool called Domain Suggestion Tool, you can still find domain names related to particular keywords that haven't been registered.

Domain Suggestion Tool http://www.domainsuggestiontool.com

You can also pick up expired domain names that still have traffic being sent to them and try to monetize the traffic. A lot of companies concentrate on buying expired domains and simply redirect them to web pages with CPA ads.

These companies are smart in that they know if they can control a vast amount of traffic with expired domains, they can convert this traffic into revenue.

Here are some resources to find expired domains:

ExpiredDomains.com http://www.expireddomains.com

DeletedDomains.com http://www.deleteddomains.com

Reciprocal Linking Traffic

Reciprocal linking is simply the link exchange between two websites. Although one-way linking helps you get a better search engine ranking, reciprocal linking still adds some benefit to your ranking.

Most people exchange links now because it helps their web site ranking, but what happened to the good old days when people used to link to each other just to exchange traffic? You will still get traffic from simple link exchanges if the links are shown prominently and not buried deep within the websites.

When trading links between websites, make sure that you are getting a fair deal of traffic for the traffic you will be giving away. It is best to use a tracking script to measure how much traffic you are sending to a link partner versus how much traffic they are sending you.

Here are a few link exchange networks where you can find quality link exchange partners.

Link Partners http://www.linkpartners.com

Value Exchange http://value-exchange.sitesell.com

FollowLike http://promoteam.rurl.me/followlike

Blogging Traffic

Blogging has become quite popular because they seem to rank quite well in search engines. Although not as effective as far as 3-5 years ago, blogs still command good rankings because of the fresh content that they bring to search engines. Blogs did well early on because of their optimized site structure. I mean if you look at a blog, it is set up with a clear navigation with every page linked correctly. This is what search engines love.

You can start your blog for free by either using a third-party blogging website or installing free blogging software on your web site.

Blogger (3rd party) http://www.blogger.com

WordPress (standalone software) http://www.wordpress.com

Another new trend in affiliate marketing is the setup of fake blogs to promote CPA offers such as Acai dieting and government grant offers. Some affiliates are creating fake personalities to create social proof for these CPA offers and trying to make it more convincing with fake comments for additional social proof.

Now, this is in no way an endorsement for this type of tactic; this is just to show you a method that is working extremely well for some CPA affiliate marketers.

Joint Venture Traffic

Joint venture traffic is a quick way to leverage the traffic sources (whether it is through email or web traffic) of other webmasters.

The reason why some product launches do well is because they have hundreds of joint venture partners promoting the same program to their email lists. This creates a stampede of traffic to the website of the product launch owner and that equates to mad sales.

If you can find joint venture partners who have highly responsive email lists, they can drive serious traffic to your website.

Most joint ventures involve an affiliate agreement where the joint venture partner takes a percent of the sale price of the product or service being promoted.

So, although joint ventures can create targeted traffic, the cost does come in the form of an affiliate commission.

If you are looking for joint venture partners, the Warrior Internet marketing forum has a section for finding joint venture partners: *Warrior Forum http://www.warriorforum.com/forum/default.asp*

Pop Up Traffic

Pop up traffic is a result of someone clicking on a pop-up window that contains an ad for your website or a pop-up window that contains your entire website.

There are hundreds of free pop up/under traffic exchanges on the Internet where you can get free pop under traffic. This traffic does not generally convert very well because these visitors are untargeted.

You will see ads from companies advertising 100,000 visitors to your website for amounts ranging from $10 - $100. This traffic is only good for increasing your web stats or Alexa ranking.

One particularly famous one is Adfly: http://promoteam.rurl.me/adfly

Video Traffic

Video traffic is quickly becoming one of the best methods to drive traffic to websites. Services such as YouTube.com have made it very easy for individuals to upload their videos and share it with their friends and the rest of the YouTube.com community.

A few years ago, many CPA affiliates took advantage of major video sites like YouTube.com by uploading videos from a variety of music artists. They were trying to promote ringtone offers within these videos, and some made a lot of money doing this.

At the end of the video, affiliates would put a message like "Get This Ringtone At" and then link to a CPA ringtone offer. The problem with this method is that they are using copyrighted videos to generate traffic to their ringtone offers and eventually YouTube.com catches on and shuts these accounts down.

This doesn't mean that you still can't use video services to generate traffic to your CPA offers. What you could simply do is first offer quality content in your videos (and this can be something as simple as a PowerPoint presentation) and link back to your money site at the end of the video.

Let me give you an example. You could create a PowerPoint presentation on how to get out of debt. You can find the material for your presentation for free on the Internet by simply googling "how to get out of debt."

Using a tool like Camtasia video, you can record the PowerPoint presentation with your voice as the audio presenting the slides. Simply link back to your money site at the end of a video promoting something related like a "debt" or a "free credit report" CPA offer.

You will generate traffic back to your money site when people go to it after watching the video and if you tag your videos properly with related terms (i.e. debt relief, credit report, debt credit score), you will move up organically on major search engines like Google, Yahoo, and MSN and get additional traffic.

You want to use keyword rich text in the title and description of your video, but yet still have a shocking or eye-catching title. Link to your video from multiple web sites to increase the link value and if you put your video on "auto- start" this will continue to generate views.

In some smaller video communities, if you generate enough views on your video, you can move up on their all-time favorite video rankings.

If you want to create more of personal touch, you can record yourself, or someone talking into the camcorder or web cam on the related topic and then pitch the CPA offer at the end of the video.

Some smart affiliates just create funny or interesting videos that are not directly related to the CPA offer. They are just hoping that their videos will go viral and be seen by a mass audience so that whatever they are pitching at the end of the video is viewed by hundreds of thousands of people.

Here are a few places where you can upload your videos for free for people to watch.

YouTube http://www.youtube.com

Google Videos http://video.google.com

Yahoo Videos http://video.yahoo.com

Viddler http://www.viddler.com

Adhysteria http://www.adhysteria.com

BoFunk http://www.bofunk.com

Esnips http://www.esnips.com

GUBA http://www.guba.com

iviewtube http://www.iviewtube.com

Kewego http://www.kewega.com

LiveVideo http://www.livevideo.com

MegaVideo http://www.megavideo.com

Metacafe http://www.metacafe.com

Motionbox http://www.motionbox.com

Myspace Videos http://vids.myspace.com

Photobucket http://www.photobucket.com

Revver http://www.revver.com

Sharkle http://www.sharkle.com

Spike http://www.spike.com

U2UpFly http://www.u2upfly.com

Vidilife http://www.vidilife.com

ViddYou http://www.viddyou.com

And if you want help making videos: try Fiverr at http://promoteam.rurl.me/fiverr

Podcast Traffic

Podcasts are audio files that are automatically delivered directly to your desktop computer, and can be transferred to a podcast. The difference is its ability to be syndicated, subscribed to, and downloaded automatically when new content is added. You can create audio files related to CPA offers and distribute them as podcasts so that they are passed onto users who are interested in the content.

For example, you could create podcasts related to celebrity gossip and promote ringtones at the end of each audio podcast.

Software Traffic

If you have any programming skills or know where to outsource cheap programmers, you could easily create a software program and spread it virally. An example would be Fiverr: http://promoteam.rurl.me/fiverr

Within the software, itself, you could promote CPA offers using banners or text links. For example, if you created a software program such as a dieting diary, you could promote dieting CPA offers with the software.

You can then upload your new software program to the many software sharing web services.

Here are just a few:

Upload.com http://upload.cnet.com

Easy-Share.com http://www.easy-share.com

Facebook Applications Traffic

Facebook allows developers to create applications to be used by the Facebook community. The potential is incredible because it offers developers the opportunity to access to the over 100 million Facebook users and make money.

A lot of developers have incorporated CPA offers into their Facebook applications and made obscene amounts of money. Some claim to have made as much as $1 million per week monetizing Facebook applications and CPA offers.

Okay, let's move on to the paid traffic sources.

PAID TRAFFIC

Pay Per Click Search Engine Traffic

Yahoo Search Marketing (formerly known as Overture and Goto) was the first successful pay per click search engine to come on to the scene in 1999.

Before 1999, many companies and individuals resisted the bid per placement idea, and that is why Open Text and AltaVista both failed in their attempts to charge advertisers for rankings a few years before Goto.com (now Yahoo Search Marketing) came onto the scene.

The reason why the market initially had resisted the idea of using a search engine that charged for placement was because they felt the results would be tainted and irrelevant.

Today, however, many pay per click search engines only allow advertisers to bid on relevant keywords to keep the quality of their search results high. For example, Google AdWords lets their users decide what ads are relevant by assigning a click-thru rate on paid advertisements.

On pay per click search engines, advertisers simply bid on keywords that are related to their product or service. Their ad listings will be displayed when a prospective customer types any of those keywords into a search form. Rankings on the major pay per click search engines are based primarily on the bid price and the click-through rate on the advertiser's ads. The nice thing about pay per click search engines is that you are in control, and you decide the maximum price you want to pay for a visitor to be directed to your web site.

Here are some of the big ad companies that will give you PPC traffic.

Google AdWords http://adwords.google.com

Yahoo Search Marketing http://searchmarketing.yahoo.com

MSN Adcenter http://adcenter.microsoft.com

Facebook http://www.facebook.com/advertising

MySpace http://advertise.myspace.com

Publisher Network Traffic

Contextual networks allow advertisers to place their text ads on thousands of websites that participate in the contextual ad network's publisher program. Most times, people refer contextual networks as mini Google AdSense services because they are the same thing.

Anytime someone clicks on an advertiser's ad on a publisher's website; the publisher is paid a percentage of the click cost. The contextual network keeps the remaining percent, and the advertiser is charged per click.

The key to driving targeted traffic from contextual networks is based on how well they can place targeted ads on the web sites in their publisher program. The better their ability to match the ads with the content on the web site, the better-quality traffic you will get.

Here are a few major contextual networks where you can buy traffic from:

Clicksor http://www.Clicksor.com

AdBrite http://www.AdBrite.com

ValidClick http://www.ValidClick.com

Pulse360 http://www.pulse360.com

Text Link Traffic

Another source of paid traffic is buying static text links on various websites. Buying static text links on websites can help you increase the number of one-way links that are pointing towards your website.

The key is to finding targeted websites that are interested in selling static links on their web site. There are web services that work as middlemen for buyers and sellers of text links.

Buying text links can help with search engine optimization by increasing your web sites rank and creating direct links for traffic back to your web site. Remember that 90% of the success of your web pages on organic search engines is related to off page factors such as the number of one-way links coming in.

Here are two major web services where you can buy static text links:

Text Link Ads http://www.Text-Link-Ads.com

Text Link Brokers http://www.TextLinkBrokers.com

Co-Registration Traffic

Co-registration is simply buying leads from companies that collect them from co- registration forms. A lot of companies can provide you with a large number of single opt-in leads on a daily basis.

Sometimes as high as 100,000 leads per day!

The price for co-registration leads varies and can start as low as $0.10 an email address. You need to take these leads and convert them into traffic. It is smart to go with a co-registration service that automatically puts these leads into an autoresponder in real-time so you can get the prospect while they are hot.

You can either direct them to your web site in an autoresponder email or try to sell directly to them in the email.

Banner Traffic

Are banners dead? Heck, no!

If you can create eye-catching banners, you can still drive a good amount of traffic to your websites. Creating text banners can out-pull image banners by up to three times.

You simply create a killer headline on your banner and try to entice the reader to click on the banner. Adding the keywords "Click Here" somewhere on your banner will almost always increase the click-thru rate.

You can literally start getting millions of banner impressions by using the site- targeting feature in Google Adwords. If you have a Google AdWords account, instead of setting up a keyword-targeting campaign, you can set up a site- targeting campaign.

You select the web sites that you want your banner to appear on, and you can test and track to see what web sites pull the best conversions for what you are promoting.

Google charges as low as $0.25 for every 1,000 banner impressions so you can test and track without losing your shirt.

Google Adwords

https://adwords.google.com

Other places where you can buy banner traffic are:

Casale Media http://www.casalemedia.com

ValueClick http://www.valueclick.com

And if you need help creating an awesome banner, try Fiverr: http://promoteam.rurl.me/fiverr

Media Buys Traffic

Media buying simply refers to buying bulk advertising space for mass advertising campaigns. You can generate a ton of traffic from doing media buys, but it can get very expensive.

The key to making media buys work well is to make sure that you have thoroughly tested the response rate of the landing page so that you have a general idea of what the conversion rate will be.

Okay, let's move on to recycled traffic…

RECYCLED TRAFFIC

Email Traffic

One of the first things that you should be concentrating on when building traffic is to have a system set up to capture email addresses of the visitors that come to your web site.

This way you can recycle this traffic by directing them back to your website through email messages. Recycled traffic is virtually free and can help brand your web site with prospects.

The first thing that you want to do is create a pop-up window on your website that grabs the attention of your visitors as soon as they arrive at your website.

Popup windows can increase your opt-in rate dramatically compared to a simple opt-in form on your web site.

As much as you may hate pop-up windows, the fact is that they work.

Internal Banner Traffic

This strategy is one of the biggest sources of recycled traffic and continues to move hundreds of visitors between network of websites every day.

This works by creating banners that only link back to websites that you own or control. This means that you are keeping your visitors on your network of websites. What this does is increase the likelihood of someone completing a CPA offer that you will be promoting on your website.

The longer you can keep traffic moving within your websites, you will see a direct relation to how much money you will make.

You can download a free script called OpenX that will completely run your internal banner network and provide you with powerful statistics on what is working and what is not.

OpenX http://www.openx.com

Forum Recycled Traffic

Forums are a great way to attract visitors back to your websites. People like to converse with each other about niche topics and will be willing to come back to your web site if you give them the ability to do so.

There are many free forum scripts on the Internet, and a perfect free one is PHP Forums, which is available at:

PHP Forum http://www.phpforum.com

You can even place banners in your forum pulled directly from the CPA networks. For example, if you are running a dieting related forum, you can run various CPA dieting offers.

Surveys and Poll Traffic

People love to express their opinion or take surveys. That is why programs that offer to pay people to take surveys do so well. By creating a poll on your website, you can encourage visitors to come back to your website to view the results. On these polls, you can run banners or text links for CPA offers.

You can create polls that are targeted towards certain CPA offers so that you are targeting the right prospects. You can go to any website that offers free CGI scripts and find a polling script fairly quickly to add to your web site. Here are some survey and poll services:

PollDaddy.com http://www.polldaddy.com

SurveyMonkey.com http://www.surveymonkey.com

Now, let's move on to one of the best and most efficient form of traffic.

VIRAL TRAFFIC

This is the most powerful form of traffic that you could generate because it is free most of the time and grows virally.

Five main pillars are the foundation for a successful viral marketing campaign:

Pillar #1: Innovative Product or Service

Viral marketing works best when you give or sell an innovative product or service that people want. Hotmail was the first web service to give away free web-based email accounts.

You don't necessarily have to reinvent the wheel; you can still give or sell a product or service that is not new and still be successful. You just will not be as successful as if you had been the first person to promote the product or service in the market.

Viral marketing programs that give away things for free usually reach the most number of people, especially if the product or service is of high-perceived value. Other common examples of valuable products and services on the Internet are free email, free eBooks, free reports, and free postcards.

Pillar #2: Ease of Transfer

A virus can only survive when it can transfer easily from one host to another. Whatever product or service you decide to promote using a viral marketing campaign, it must be easily transferable.

For example, chain letters thrive on the Internet because they can easily be transmitted via email. Digital products such as e-books, reports, and software programs spread like wildfire because they are easy to copy and transfer.

Pillar #3: Motivational Factor

The product or service must motivate the user to pass it on to others. For example, electronic greeting cards thrive on viral marketing because people are motivated to send greeting cards to each other.

Numerous motivational behaviors can be exploited with viral marketing strategies to ensure the transmission of a marketing message. One of the most common motivational factors is the opportunity to make money. This is why many network marketing companies have become successful.

Pillar #4: Third-Party Resources

Viral marketing campaigns take advantage of other people's resources. For example, authors who give away free e-books or software and allow users to spread them around are taking advantage of other people's resources.

It is the user who is paying for the list server and bandwidth costs when he or she sends out these free e-book or software to their ezine.

Pillar #5: Scalability

The failure of many companies that run a viral marketing campaign is the fact that they could not scale from small to large quickly enough, killing the host in the end.

For example, at one point, Hotmail could not handle all the email accounts that were being registered and used. They simply did not have the resources to manage the explosion in new accounts.

There is a good chance that they could have ended up going out of business if Microsoft had not bought them out and infused their resources into the Hotmail service.

This is also the primary reason why a lot of hit exchanges and banner exchanges crashed in the past. They could not handle the bandwidth on their servers, and their services ultimately came to a screeching halt - causing many of their users to abandon them.

If you create a viral marketing campaign that is dependent on your resources, you must plan ahead to handle additional growth.

Developing a viral marketing campaign will be pointless if it ends up killing the host while it expands exponentially.

Social Networking Traffic

Websites like MySpace.com and YouTube.com command enormous amounts of traffic because of their users. They have created social networks that allow people to get in touch with each other more easily and share items such as videos.

The thing that makes these websites so powerful is that they are completely user driven. It is the community that builds that website and content. It is the users that are spreading the message and telling their friends to join the community. This is the viral aspect of social networking websites.

If you are serious about starting your social networking site that grows virally, you can get free scripts on the Internet that will allow you to build your own mini Myspace. Once you build your community, you can place targeted CPA offers and generate CPA commissions from all the free traffic.

Ning http://www.ning.com

Dolphin Smart Community Builder http://ww.boonex.com/products/dolphin

For a thorough guide on Social Media Marketing, check out my ebook *"Social Media Marketing: Proven Strategies To Make Big Money Online"* at this link:
https://www.amazon.com/dp/B074WGKMHR

Tell A Friend Script Traffic

"Tell a friend" scripts are a powerful viral marketing tool because it encourages people to let their friends know about your website. People are more inclined to visit your web site when a trusted friend recommends it to them.

If you have your website, you should take advantage of a script like this because you can promote your CPA offers within emails that are sent out from the script and capture more leads.

FreeTellAFriend.com http://www.freetellafriend.com

Viral Report Traffic

Many people create reports and give them away hoping that people will pass them around. Some offer resells rights, and others grant users permission to give them away for free or use them as bonuses for their products. This report that you are reading is a prime example of a viral report.

CHAPTER 7: WHY DO SO MANY CPA AFFILIATE MARKETERS FAIL?

You're ready to quit your day job – tell your boss to take a hike and head on over to the online world to take advantage of internet marketing. You sit into the wee hours of the morning obsessed. Everything sounds amazing from Facebook money making to email marketing to making money on YouTube. It makes sense to you, so you buy a course. This is like the gold rush of the 1800s and you are about to strike it rich - The next thing you know, your brain runs out of room for the clutter, your wallet is empty and your dream dies before it ever gets off the ground. Yet you could have avoided all of this. You really could have struck gold – so what did you do wrong?

You Quit Too Soon – It's Also What CPA Marketers Do Far Too Often

If you don't buy a ticket to the lottery, you can't win. Never have truer words been said. The prize for internet marketing isn't just big – it's huge – its life changing. If you want to succeed, you need to 'never say die.' That attitude will guarantee that you will eventually enjoy success. Hang on to your day job for a little longer, put your energy into getting your CPA marketing off the ground, and then you will be ready to quit with success already in your pocket.

Running before You Walk

In other words, excess rush, which will reduce your chances of making decent money online. It's much better to work towards making and extra $20 a day than to go too BIG right from the beginning, spreading yourself too thin because you believe that you need to be making $100 a day right now! Slow and steady really does win the online race. That's how you will enjoy successful CPA marketing.

Is Your CPA Marketing Actually Working?

If you want to be successful working online, you need to be ready to test and tweak everything you do in an ongoing fashion. It's common for newbies in the CPA marketing world to be reckless and this often results in some profit, but the problem is that you aren't able to pinpoint just how or why you made the money so it's impossible to duplicate your results. You need to be smarter than that – you need to keep good notes. Try something – wait – evaluate.

CPA Marketing Done Right Means Success

Do it right, take your time, be patient, be flexible and you can enjoy CPA Marketing success.

CHAPTER 8: 6 STEPS TO CHOOSE THE BEST CPA OFFER TO PROMOTE

If you want to create the best CPA offer to promote, follow these six steps.

Step #1

Picking a niche that you think you can promote takes a little strategy. It's good to choose a niche that you have some knowledge in, because this can help to reduce the time it takes to get going. If you aren't sure at the beginning, don't worry, you will develop this skill you need over time. If you are new to this, I would recommend that you look for something in the payout range of $2 to $10. This will help keep your testing cheap. The last thing you need to consider is the source of your traffic. Some traffic sources will not allow some types of offers or they might not do well with a certain offer.

Step #2

Find your niche and then seek out the top offers that have on average the highest network EPCs. List the top few offers on the CPA networks you have joined. You shouldn't compare network average EPCs between the various CPA networks. There are far too many variables and so your comparisons will not be valid or provide you with good insight.

Step #3

Your affiliate managers are there to help you and to answer your questions. One of the thing you need to ask is what offers your affiliate manager feels is doing the best in your particular niche.

Step #4

Take the time to have a look at each offer in-depth. Look at things like the design, the landing page copy, the consumer price; if it is a direct sale offer and just how you feel overall about the design. What is your gut feeling? Take advantage of Alexa.com, where you can check out how much traffic the offer URL gets. This information can help you tell if the offer is new or if it's been around for some time. Being new should not be a deal breaker but it is something to be aware of and to pay attention to. Think about how easily or quickly you can make a good landing page.

Step #5

Pick two or three top offers that you are going to split test. It is important that you test each offer for a minimum of 100 clicks before you make any decisions.

Step #6

This step is only necessary if your offer requires you to have approval. You will then need to reach out to the affiliate manager or the person that approves the applications. Don't be afraid to pick up the phone and call them as a follow up to your approval request. Almost all are going to call you to ensure you are a legitimate business, so beat them to it. Answer all questions you are asked, or perhaps, if you have any questions too, they would be willing to help.

CHAPTER 9: HOW TO JOIN A CPA NETWORK

Joining a CPA Network is more difficult than joining a basic market affiliating program. But if you know how this system works, you can certainly create your own opportunity especially using these steps:

#1 Choose one or more networks that you would like to join. You definitely want to choose more than one CPA Network. There is a wide collection of networks to choose and apply (You can even refer to the Chapter 5 section of this book) in order to land up with the best offers, since more applications means an increase in your options. Make sure that you take the time to compare the options and features of each of the networks since different networks will have different pay for the same offers. Choose the network that best seems to suits your needs.

#2 Fill out the submission form and try your best to answer all the questions as best that you can. The network managers are interested in knowing about your website, how much traffic you generate, the methods you wish to use to make online sales, etc. Don't be scared by these questions. Just be honest. If you have extremely limited knowledge in this business scope, it will not be the end of the world. They realize that you have to start somewhere, so just be honest in answering the questions.

#3 After you submit the forms, expect to wait for a week or sometimes even longer before you hear from anyone. If you want to speed things up, all you need to do is give the CPA network a call and you watch how quickly you get approved to their CPA network! When the managers see how enthusiastic you are to get the job, they will be impressed enough to have you working for them immediately!

#4 You might discover that some CPA networks are difficult to join. In these situations, it is better that you tell them what your business plan looks like to promote their offers. This will allow them to see that you have the initiative to make sure everything is in order. This will make them far more likely that they accept you right away!

In rare occasion where these tricks fail to work, you can have a successful CPA marketer put a good word in for you. Begin to work in those networks that you have been accepted, and then you can begin to build more experience. It doesn't hurt to build on your contacts. Before you know it, you will start to work as a CPA marketer!

Business is all about making money. So as long as you can keep the green flowing to a business, they'll be interested in having you on board.

CHAPTER 10: THE #1 FEAR IN CPA MARKETING

You are reading this because you want to know what the main fear is when it comes to CPA marketing. If you are new to CPA marketing, it can be kind of scary. Don't let the fear of you losing your money be the reason for stopping yourself from making money. Success is really based on making sure you **test – test – test** – stay on top of what you are doing, know what's working and what's not working.

The fear of failure is the number one fear in CPA marketing. It's also what will stop most people dead in their tracks before they even get started. After all, if you haven't started, you can't fail, of course, you also can't succeed. Having this mentality is not the mentality for success.

Perhaps it's due to lack of self confidence, or maybe you have low self esteem. Whatever the reason, you need to address it if you want to enjoy success in CPA marketing. You need to be patient and you need to be willing to step out of your comfort zone. Chances are for most of you considering CPA marketing as beginners, it's something you've not done before. So it's going to take some time for you to be comfortable. The reality is that you are likely to fail your first go round at CPA marketing. After all, you really do need to be bad before you can be good and then when you really understand the 'game' you'll be great. Keep this in mind. It's part of your journey to success.

The message here is if at first you don't succeed and you fail, don't walk away. Get back up, dust yourself off, and try again! Can you imagine what the world would be like if we were all successful the first time we tried something? The thing is that many will fail and then never try again. Instead, they'll head back to the life they know. What you need to remember is that you are working towards a goal, towards successful CPA marketing that can create a steady income flow for you and change your life. The best way for you to deal with your strong fear of failure is to have a very strong focus. When you have something that you are working towards with purpose, it will help to keep you motivated and you will be much less likely to quit.

CPA marketing has great potential; don't let fear stop you from experiencing the revenue it can generate.

CHAPTER 11: THE BENEFITS OF CPA MARKETING

CPA marketing – if you aren't familiar with it now is a good time to learn more about it. You may have used Google AdSense or perhaps you have used sites like Clickbank. If you are unhappy with the results, you aren't alone. CPA marketing is different, and it is one of the best as an affiliate that you can monetize your site(s).

CPA or Cost Per Action Marketing is a simple system. When someone clicks on your affiliate link and he/she completes the necessary action, you get paid. The necessary action, can be many different things, but usually involves:

* Getting a quote or estimate

* Filling out a form

* Buying something

* Signing up for a free trial

These are the main actions required for you to get paid with CPA Marketing. But why should you choose CPA marketing over some of the other options? Glad you asked!

Why Use CPA Marketing

There are two key reasons to consider using CPA Marketing rather than AdSense, banner advertising or other affiliate marketing strategies. The most important is simply that you are higher on the value chain and the higher the value the more money you are likely to make from your site. That means you'll see higher ROI on CPA Marketing than you will on other forms of marketing. Physical products have up to ten different companies involved in that product, such as warehouses, distributors, and suppliers. It's why if you are an Amazon Associate selling a $3000 computer, you only make about $100.

The second reason to consider CPA Marketing is that it is an integrated form of advertising. That means there is no need for you to make your site look ugly with banner ads and AdSense blocks. CPA Marketing will seamlessly integrate with your site. The offers fit in with your content and blends in with your site. This means that you can easily run a branded website that looks clean and professional, while you can still benefit from CPCs, RPMs, and CTR.

CPR Marketing provides you with a seamless way to integrate advertising. You start by finding an offer that you are interested in and that you feel will work well with your website. There are all kinds of CPA networks out there; each has hundreds of different offers, so you should not have a problem finding an offer that works well with your site.

CONCLUSION

CPA Marketing is really that simple. You just pick an offer, drive traffic to the offer or landing page and when a conversion is performed, you get paid.

Don't overcomplicate CPA marketing and just take one step at a time.

The "Biggest Secret" to succeeding as a CPA Marketer is to always test!

You need to test different networks, different offers, different landers, different traffic sources and pretty much test everything you possibly can.

Here's hoping you have learnt a lot from this guide, and it's time to implement every step.

Stay Awesome!
Jerry Shoemaker

www.ingramcontent.com/pod-product-compliance
Lightning Source LLC
Chambersburg PA
CBHW031515210526
45464CB00007B/2917